CW00405105

Copyright © 2021 Jessica Smithers-Jones

All rights reserved.

ISBN: 9798404050370

DEDICATION

To my boys, I thank you giving me the gift of being a mum.
To my mum for always supporting my dreams.
To Alisha for finding yourself.
To Graham, for always loving me for who I am.
You are my favourite.

CONTENTS

The Stories

ACKNOWLEDGMENTS

To all the other female authors who have pathed a way for other
women to speak their truth.
I thank you deeply.

This book has been written to help you understand your internal connection with source/spirit/higher self.
To help you run a soul lead business which lights up your life, fills up your bank account and brings you multiple orgasms!

From periods to payment systems, we've got you covered.
But we must start at the beginning of this story to help you get to the end of your dreams.

Get turned on and tap into your wildest desires.

YOUR PUSSY, YOUR BUSINESS

THE BLEEDING.

How I begin this book will never truly matter, because it's what you take away with you at the end of the book is what counts. I love a good book as much as the next person. In fact, reading and writing for a long time whilst growing up was my way to escape reality, to escape everything and enter a world of incredible possibilities. As I began to grow older, I would write small stories, a page or two long. I would write about my day in my diary and feel bliss as the pen touched the paper. Lost in the words as my handwriting began to change into a scribbled mess as more words were floating through my mind faster than I could write down. Even when exhausted I wouldn't stop, fighting through the wrist ache, the blurry eyes. I would write and yet not even know where these words came from or what they even meant a lot of the time.

As I found myself in secondary school and the pressure of society hitting me, writing became a distant friend, days become weeks, and weeks become months. Those months become years of self-hate, self-doubt and bunking off school to do, not a lot really. None of my friends ever spoke about writing things down, and even when I asked them, they would make fun of it, so in a desperate plea to fit in, from the age of 12 I stopped writing completely, apart from the mandatory schoolwork and homework, but I cut myself off from my imagination. I didn't write from my soul anymore.

Luckily, all that began to change as I began to find myself again, at the age of 22 I began to journal again and even whilst I was in the Army, I began to write short stories. I never believed in myself enough that I would be able to actually have my own book, I had thought about it for years, I would type up a chapter then leave it for months, never wanting to go back to it, but here we are with a BOOK!!!

The thought of sitting at a computer just wasn't as satisfying as writing it all down. So, after almost 4 years of trying to type up my book, I have hand-written my book, I wrote it all out, allowing myself to flow and for the right words to come to me, from my higher self. I allowed myself to write it all before I ever sat in-front of the computer to type it all up. That's where the magic happened for me, allowing the space inside my mind to come out onto paper, to allow myself to disappear into the words that flowed from my heart to my hand and into the pen, from the pen to the ink, from the ink to the paper. Even the thought of thinking words and our body being able to move in the perfect way to produce the words for others to know and understand blows my mind.

How incredibly powerful we are.

As women being able to read and write so freely here in the UK is truly a blessing that so many of us have taken for granted over the years.

When I think back to when women weren't allowed to read or write, it must have been so frustrating for them, to not be able to fully express themselves. All the authors who were never able to fulfil their destinies, all the teachers who were never able to teach because they couldn't read. Or all the powerful women, witches who could not read nor write spells. The knowledge of the woman that was lost over centuries.

We often forget how far we have come to be able to freely read and write our thoughts, even if it's just on a sticky note or posting a short tweet, to writing blog posts and even books.

We are so blessed to be able to have so much, that those that came before us fought for us to have, things they couldn't even imagine, we have today.

As I feel so insanely blessed to be able to not only read and write but to have the freedom to write what my soul calls me to do, I have even added a few saucy short stories at the back of this book for you to enjoy. I love writing erotica, it excites me. The way my whole body comes alive as I write is so trilling to me, and I hope as you read these short stories you too connect with yourself, allowing yourself to drift off and connect to your pussy, your needs, and desires.

When I got the idea to share the short stories in this book, I was out walking my dog and planting some blood magic. I figured if the idea was calling, I will answer the call.

That's what this book is about. It's about us answering the call to live our lives to the fullest. No more half assed bull shit.

Instead living to what our souls are calling us to do. Share parts of ourselves that lead us to be open and vulnerable. Me writing about my vulnerabilities and mistakes and wins is what makes me, me. I have fucked up a lot in my life, but I have also done some pretty amazing things too. So, if I am called to write stories that will help women connect to their pussy and potentially have insane orgasms from the stories then so be it. If you chose not to read them, that's also awesome to. I used to worry so much about what I could write about, and who would read it, would it be liked or even appropriate. Now as I get closer to my 30th birthday I think sod it all. However…

Nan if you read this book, just remember I love you, and probably avoid the back section, haha.

 Mum you already know who I am, better than anyone, so thanks for giving me the courage to write it all.

 Have you ever looked back and noticed where your cut off point was, from yourself? Where you were no longer a child, free to play and be creative, but instead follow the conditions of society in order to fit in?

When asking questions made you feel weird and misunderstood? That brings me onto the biggest topic of this book.

Knowing your periods and your bodies but mostly yourself. Collectively as one big ball of amazingness.

For me this all began in year 7 aged 12. Where I lost my inner child and stepped into my newfound role, as a woman who had periods, which may I add - scared the shit out of me.

 There were whispers of people in the school who had just started their periods, and girls who still hadn't. The pressure of starting your periods meant people saw you as more than before, yet also disgusted that your pussy was a red demon. If you hadn't had your period yet, you were slow and taunted for 'not having a clue how 'it' feels'. It didn't take long for me to start mine, I'm not sure if it was the collective energy of always being around older girls that caused it, but when it happened. I felt more accepted by my friends yet also disgusted in my body.

When I told my mum I was bleeding, she was happy for me, in just a casual way. We went together to buy some period pads, and I remember getting so overwhelmed at the size of some of those things. Right from the start of my periods I was a heavy bleeder. My mum grabbed the delightful 'heavy flow' pads. It was like wearing a nappy on top of a nappy. "How the hell did women deal with this?" I remember thinking to myself. I felt embarrassed by the size of the thing, and so self-conscious that you could see the line where the pad stopped. I used to pull my jumper down as far as it would go in attempts to hide the damn thing.

I hated everything about it, the pad size, the smell, the blood still all over my pussy and my legs where it hadn't soaked into the pad. I was 12, 2 or 3 periods in and I was done. I wanted off the period train. I had my ticket, and I was ready to check out.

No more. Nope. Done! Done!! DONE!!

"I wanted off the period train"

One day in the toilets a friend offered me a tampon, and still to this day I have never seen a tampon like it.

I stared at it blankly 'What the hell do I do with this?' I asked her. 'Push it into that side of the packet, it has lube in there. Then you take it out and push it up inside of you." She giggled as she walked into the toilet cubicle. I walked into the cubicle next to her and followed her instructions.

Holy crap! It was horrible. The damn thing wouldn't get out of the lube, then my fingers were all sticky. I was terrified it would get lost inside of me, so I only pushed it up until I could still feel it at the base. **BAD IDEA**.

Walking to class was one of the most uncomfortable walks ever but sitting down was a whole different story. I was so uncomfortable, I was adjugated and flustered. I wanted it out, and I wanted it out then and there. After a painful 50-minute class, the bell rang and I stumbled my way to the bath room to rip that beast out of me. I felt like something was wrong with me. I had over-heard all the other girls talking about tampon, how clean and easy it was. I thought my pussy was broken. Now I know it was perfect, I just hadn't fully understood the instructions and with lack of guidance and understand my self-worth in that moment was at rock bottom.

I know now that if that happened to me, it must have happened to other women, and will continue to happen to more women. Not only do I know this is true from my school experience but when I was 20, I went to work abroad on a private yacht – that's a whole different story.

The chef on board was a female in her early 30's. One day she asked me if I had any pads as she had a surprise visit from mother nature. At that point I was queen of the tampons and had mastered it. I offered her one, and she had that same look I had as a 12-year-old girl. This 30-year-old Russian woman looked like a scared little girl. I held her hand and walked her to the bathroom. I talked her through it step by step. I told her different positions she could stand/sit in to make the application more comfortable for her and asked if she could feel it afterwards. I reminded her it was safe to have it up inside of her, and that she shouldn't feel it in the dropped down position. When she came out of the bathroom, she hugged me so tightly and began to well up. She didn't have to say anything, but I knew how much that meant to her. Not everyone has women around to talk about these things, or even be a friend on the other side of the door.

Growing up we are told to be quiet about our periods, don't ask questions. Expected to just 'know' how it all works because it's our bodies.

I want you to go back to when you first started to bleed, remember how it made you feel. What was happening around you? Were you free to ask questions to adult women or were you left to your group of friends – also new to periods – to work it all out?

How do you treat your periods today? Do you feel like you are safe to ask questions? Do you feel safe in your body and held by the women around you, during your bleed?

By the age of 14 my periods were crippling me, I would be sick, in agony, and there were several occasions where I would bleed through my clothes in class. I hated it. I hated every part of being a girl. It sucked. I eventually went to tell my mum how heavy the periods were, and I got booked in to see the doctor. He didn't ask me many questions as soon as the words 'painful periods' were mentioned he turned to his computer and printed off a prescription for the pill. I tried my best to remember to take them, but I am not the best at remembering things. I set alarms, had them next to my bed, placed them by the kettle, yet I could still go days, even weeks without taking it, my periods become more irregular and soon enough I was having a period every 2 weeks.

I read an article that mentioned how having sex can reduce period pains. I didn't know how, and I was still a virgin but again the pressure of society was hitting me hard. There were several girls already in my year group that had lost their virginities and I began to feel the urge to follow suit. Most girls talked about having a romantic first time, all the films I had watched were making a big deal out of it too. But I knew it was going to be painful blood bath. I did not want to share that experience with someone I loved. It didn't feel precious to me, I just wanted to get it over and done with so I could get to the pleasure state where sex could stop my periods from hurting me. It didn't take long for me to find a boy that would sleep with me, I wasn't a 10 but I wasn't a 5 either, possibly a comfortable 7, 8 at a push on a good day.

We had arranged everything, he was going to come to my house, and get it over and done with. He kept asking if it meant that we were 'together' but I kept dismissing him. I didn't want him to know I was just using him to get what I wanted – which also become the way I lived my life for a very long time. My first time pretty much set me up for my relationships for 10 years.

Use and abuse. Sometimes I did the using, sometimes I was the used and abused.

At my house, my bedroom was tiny, as the bigger rooms were used for guests to stay in, my mum and dad owned a 6 bedroom Guest house, with additional bedrooms for us. I lay my bedding on the floor and laid down. He put on the condom and we began.

My whole body was in pain, excruciating pain. I remember closing my eyes and thinking to myself 'it will be okay. Next time will be better'.

When it was over, I saw he was covered in blood, and so was I. I grabbed my dressing gown and ran to the bathroom. Every step was as if I was being stabbed, and I could feel the blood running down my legs. I got in the shower and cried. In fact, I sobbed. I felt disgusted. I hated my body. I hated the blood. I hated the smell. I eventually got out the shower and went back to my room to find he was still there. I was so wrapped up in my thoughts, I had completely forgotten he was there. He looked unsettled, as I saw the blood still all over him, on his belly, on his legs, on his hands, his privates. I grabbed him a towel and showed him to the shower. By the time he had got back I was in my pj's with clean sheets on the bed, I asked him to get his stuff and leave. I didn't see him again after that first time. I felt like I had betrayed my body, I felt dirty, and the pain in my womb only got worse. I felt so embarrassed, the bleeding continued to dominate my life, but I kept going back to that article. Now I had my first time out the way, surely it would get better, right?

And so it began, my long slippery slope to SlutVile. I began to sleep around with different guys, but the results were always the same. I would either bleed during sex, or straight after, but sex was always painful. It didn't matter how big or small the guy was, it hurt. It hurt really bad.

My view already from my tampon incident was that my pussy was broken, and now having sex was just reaffirming to me, that indeed my pussy was broken. I didn't dare talk to anyone about it, and none of the guys I slept with mentioned the bleeding either. I was relieved, I got used to being called a slut, but in my eyes, I wasn't a slut. I was just desperate to find that sex that fixes you like the article said. I was desperate to not be broken. I was desperate to understand my own body.

I was scared of my womanhood. I hated being a woman. I hated not knowing about my body and why I behaved the way I did.

LISTENING TO SELF

When I was 15, I met a guy. The tall, dark and handsome type. The bad boy. I wanted him and I got him, except there was one thing different about this guy. Our sex was different. It was hungry and thirsty. Like tasting something amazing for the first time and never being able to stop. It consumed me. At first sex was slightly painful but the longer we went the less it hurt. The less it hurt the more I wanted of it.

Have you ever had that type of sex? Where your pussy purrs at every single touch?

After a few weeks the period pains were less, the bleeding was more to a normal cycle, and I had become obsessed. I had unleashed something inside of me, and she was not about to be put back into the shadows.

Several months went by and we were blissfully happy, my pussy and I were also on great terms. Until things began to unravel. He was cheating on me with several people.

It was the beginning of a road to hell. A road in which I walked daily and came out the other side several years later.

From the moment I was cheated on the pain came back, I kept taking him back and the bleeding began again, the pain during and after sex worsened. I now know this was my inner Goddess telling me to get out, that she wasn't being worshipped and if I didn't leave on her demand, shit was going to hit the fan. I didn't listen, so that's exactly what happened.

Have you ever experienced when life just seems out of your control?

Shit happens that you never even saw coming, even though you had all the warning signs in the first place, but you choose to ignore them?

Then felt even more hurt, that even after the warnings, the shit still came?

I wish I knew back then what I know now about my Goddess within. She is stubborn, loud, demanding, but sensitive and hidden. She is ME and I am her. The only difference between us both is she has a deeper knowing of what's going on in my life and what's going to happen in my life. She is 5 steps ahead, on a higher level of vibration giving me the warning signs. It's my job to either listen or fuck up and beg for guidance.

I ask you now, are you listening?

Or are you begging for guidance?

I begged for a long time, I begged for the answers, to which I already knew the answers to, but I didn't want to listen to those answers. I wanted to hear the opposite. I wanted to hear the happy ever after, but the more I pushed against her truth, the more pain and suffering I went through.

The more I pushed, the harder the push back was. I was exhausted, beaten, and broken. Until one day it all came to a crashing halt.

That day, everything I knew came crashing down around me, and I was free but extremely damaged. For a long time, I struggled with trust and infidelity in relationships. Not only from other people, but from myself to. I would go out of my own way to ruin a relationship that seemed 'good'. I'd push people away and hide my emotions, building up a wall to keep myself safe.

We experience these types of moments not only in our personal relationships but also in our business.

Have you ever had the idea to run a new course or sell a new product? You keep pushing, trying different ways to make it work. Your body feels off about it all but in your head, you still think there is a way to make it work? But it just doesn't come through and by the end you have used up your savings, you feel like a failure and your moral is well and truly crushed.

Hidden away from your business and finances, just so you don't have to be real and honest with yourself or your accountant? Sabotaged yourself, your business, your relationships?

These moments may feel like the end of the world and honestly, they are. They are the end of that world. That should also be something we celebrate, maybe not at the time but you can always look back and celebrate the death of that world as it created space to birth the world you live in now – or your future world. Take some time to journal and think back to when you have stopped yourself in life or business because someone you loved broke your trust, and you acted out of pain.

Pain gives us lessons, but if we aren't open to knowing these lessons then we repeat that cycle, but when we understand where our behaviour has come from we can forgive that person and move on. Leaving the pains and struggle behind us and creating room in our lives to act differently.

You may have experienced similar times in your life, feel like you are having to push through. Fighting to make a relationship work, holding on for dear life.

To quote Pink – white knuckles, and sweaty palms from hanging on to tight. Clenched shut jaw, I've got another headache again tonight.

It often feels like we're drowning in the relationship, desperate to make it work. This isn't always a relationship with another person. This could also be the relationship you have with your job or business, self.
Regardless of where it is that you are holding on so tight, this is your time to let it go.

To learn to listen to your higher self.
To your inner guidance system.
To your Goddess.
To your pussy.

Forgiving someone who broke your trust or hurt you could feel like an impossible task, but you have already survived the destruction. The forgiveness isn't for them, nor do you have to do it directly to them. The forgiveness is for you. For you to move forward and call in more beauty in the space opened from letting go.

"white knuckles, and sweaty palms from hanging on to tight"
- Pink.

Yes, it is fucking scary (*emphasis on the fucking*) but do you know what is even scarier? Having someone else take your world from under your feet, or even worse having your grip to tight you suffocate and kill it off.

When every fiber of your body is feeling exhausted with the fight, it is not an invitation for you to jump in deeper, it's an invitation for you to walk away and release it.

For you to come back to yourself.

Over the years I have walked away from countless lovers who couldn't give me what I required, as painful as it was all those encounters lead me to make decisions I never would have taken before – like joining the British Army. Where I met my husband or like giving up on different business adventures because they were draining me, and I was investing so much money into them and never getting a return. Yet if I had never taken those risks at the time, I wouldn't now have the knowledge I do today, and I wouldn't have a business that is smooth and tailored to me and my needs, but also to the needs of my family and my clients. Taking that leap of faith on letting go has often felt like I was giving up on myself, on my dreams and sometimes even giving up on other people or letting them down. I know that letting go of these things that keep us stuck, actually benefits us in the long run. It allows us to create space for more things to come our way. Things that we were never expecting like money, opportunities and new relationships that are deeper and more meaningful. At the time is doesn't always feel like something good is going to come from that, but over the years I've learnt that nervous feeling is usually an indication we have made the right decision and something better is on the way. If you still feel unsure or it feels like a big decision to be made, drop into your pussy. The best time to do it is during menstruation, this is when the veil is thinner, and you are able to hear your inner Goddess more.

Your menstruation is a time of coming inwards, to listen. To feel and know. We talk more about this in the Cycle Section.

Listening to that whisper can lead us on journey we never would have expected or tried to create for ourselves. It's the whisper to pick up a new book or go into a shop or even go down a different street or career change. For me that little whisper came one day in the form of going on holiday, then stopping at a shop, to finding a book hidden. The shop keeper didn't even realise she had that book for sale. But there it was, with a price tag on the back, in my hands. This book caused big shifts to happen within me. I began to learn about ancient ways of being a woman. When I first found out about these old ways of being, it was like my body felt so sad and small, like I hadn't truly been celebrated for who I was. So, I took matters into my own hands!

I took myself off contraceptive, I had an IUD for roughly 14 years, only being off it to conceive then immediately having an IUD rammed back up there to ensure I didn't get pregnant again.

I made the bold move and had it out. I wanted to allow my body to have a period again. I told myself this time it would be different. This time they won't cripple me, and so far, I have had beautiful cycles. My first period from the removal of the IUD felt like I had been caged for years and for the first time in years I felt free. It took my breath away. My energy was so different, I conducted myself differently. I felt like a woman. All of the knowledge my ancestors had come flooding to me, I felt like I had generations of women stood by me and behind me cheering me on.

Bleeding freely with me.

On my second bleed I decided I was going to give myself a

menarche ceremony. It was small and personal to me, and I did what my body called me to do. I wore a red dress throughout the day, and in the evening, I ran myself a hot bath, crystals lined one side of the bath and I picked several different shapes from the curvy candle collection to represent women in my life and the women that came before me. I played a sound bath audio and lit a jar candle, blood red from the woman's collection. I placed a small dot of my blood on my 3rd eye, and I said out loud "I am me, I am them, I am she". I repeated this 3 times as I lowered myself into the bath. I honored myself, those who came before me and after me, and the Goddesses.

You don't have to do the same ritual as me, you can simply have a bath and just tell yourself you are safe in your period, in your body. You could simply light a candle and sit with it or have a huge ceremony with other women and all celebrate and dance. Congratulate each other for having periods and bask in the beauty that is available to you. If the thought of having a ceremony lights your heart on fire but don't feel you have women around you to do this with, you can always join us on a Red Tent Weekend Retreat.

We host 1 retreat a year but keep an eye out on our website – **_curvyco.uk_** for more information and dates.

Just like in business we need to surround ourselves with positive like-minded people. People to encourage us, to cheer us on when we don't always feel like it. To give us guidance and support. We seek to build up our business empires but it's not a task one can do alone. In business we have times of celebrations and times of reflection, but to celebrate alone isn't as fun as celebrating with the people around you cheering you on. We have systems and rituals in business, we can also have them for sex and self-care.

It was always a dream of mine to host a retreat, to be able to bring women together into a space where they can be free to truly be themselves. To not feel shamed for being a woman, for not having to feel embarrassed by anything and for them to just know, no matter what they have done or been through in life, they are loved.

For me this big journey of bringing women together stemmed from moving around a lot and not feeling like I had friends to rely on. Being in the Army friendship groups were very clicky, and not many people were into the spiritual side of things. So, I often felt very alone and spent most of the time by myself.

In the online space I felt like I saw so many women growing and expanding in their business, I would cheer others on but there was always that personal connection missing. It's easier to create friendships online, but they don't always have that magic that real life in person connections have. There is nothing like the magic of making new friends and sharing a very sacred space with each other.

When I got my first foster child, she had to move away from her friends, although she was commuting to her usual school where her friends attended the thought of making new friends where she lived was terrifying for her. In fact, it was for me to. We moved to Chester a week before she came to live with us. I didn't have any friends when I first moved here, but just like with anything in life, the more you put yourself out there and connect to your true self, the more the universe aligns with that and will bring you people or events to help you step into more.

I also know I am not alone when it comes to feeling alone, the feeling of not being able to make friends or have close friendships with people isn't only experienced by me, but by hundreds of women, all over the world.

We yearn for women we can be close with, to build communities with women, to be able to support each other and be there for each other. To make life easier with each other. But we have been silenced so much, the thought of trying to reach new people to make friends stops us in our tracks.

This is also felt in business when we are trying to attract new clients to our business. We yearn to have deep impactful relationships with our clients, to support them and watch them grow. It's my favourite thing about working closely with women. It's the deep relationships that are created. It's the healing of the sister wounds, the witch wounds, the divide in community.

To many are just about the money, they lose touch of the importance of other people. For many we step into the space of online coaching to reach more women/men across the world, but it feels empty when we don't have those strong connections in our lives.

We can often feel ashamed of who we are or that we don't have friendship circles or people in our lives that understand our calling to our higher selves, so in order to not sound crazy or feel uncomfortable we stay hidden and lonely.

When we feel called to go to new places or do new things, we can get stuck in our heads, often referred to as anxiety. I've come to learn that the anxiety we feel is our heads talking us out of what our soul is calling us to do.

Listening to ourselves can be hard, uncomfortable but ohh so rewarding when we do.

I had to listen to the calling to finally sit and write.

I had to listen to my environments when they were falling down around me.

I had to listen to my body when all I wanted to do was ignore things or push through.

I had to listen when my old businesses weren't working and I had to change direction even though I was scared.

I had to listen when I was called to take responsibility over my finances and I had to take that daily action.

I share this because I know how scary it can be to listen to your soul, when your head is shouting even louder.

I found through meditation it became easier to listen to my soul rather than my head. I'm a huge believer in – Meditation does not mean a quiet mind.

Instead, I like to see it as a way to shift through the shouting to find the inspirational whispers. It's more sifting and sorting rather than quieting.

Meditation has been disguarded by most in the western world, "it's bullshit" I hear a lot of people say.

Honestly for a long time I was one of those people, I'd rather get blacked out drunk to deal with my shit than have to sit in silence with my own thoughts. But whilst I didn't sit with myself, my life was falling apart all around me.

Now I do sit with myself, my life has changed dramatically. If you feel that you'd like to do meditations but don't know where to start, I invite you to join our Facebook community where I host guided meditations – ***Sacred Women in Business – CurvyCo***

FINDING YOUR VOICE

For a long time, I felt I didn't have a voice, being told to be quiet was a big influence in my life, I grew up in a B&B where the guests had to come first. I had to be quiet sneaking around in the morning getting ready for school. My alarms had to be quiet so not to wake anyone else up. I would have to be quiet going down 2 flights of stairs to use the bathroom. I had to be quiet to not disturb the peace of others. I hated it, I liked loud music, and wanted to walk around as and when I pleased. I hated being told to be quiet, yet as I've grownup I don't like noise, it feels like chaos to me.

Our voices can be lost well before our first periods, so when we step into adulthood and decide to run our own business, often we aren't heard or misunderstood or have fears of public speaking. From getting your periods to speaking your truth can be a long journey, but when you find your voice in the ocean of noise, it's sweet to the ears.

For some of you, your first period could have been many moons ago. For some not as many. Everyone's journey is different and perfectly unique to them.

Realizing how you were made to feel at that moment of stepping into woman hood shapes you as a woman. It's the foundations to how you grow up seeing yourself.

If you were shamed into it, told not to speak of it, told 'women don't discuss periods or sex' 'those subjects are dirty', then I'm pretty sure unless you have done a lot of healing work around that, you still move every month through your cycle with the same shame. Even if you have transitioned from your periods to menopause, those feelings will still be there in your everyday life.

If you were taught how to love your periods and your body, talk about periods and sex openly then you will most likely carry less shame.

Having the freedom to discuss the subjects doesn't always mean the freedom was there to have those conversations with grown women who can give you guidance and support.

It can feel easy to look around and blame people, judge people, be jealous of people for their openness, their lack of fear of speaking out on subjects that matter to them. If you find yourself scrolling through social media checking out what others are doing then chances are you will sometimes feel envious of other women being on camera, talking, doing their thing. Notice where that sits with you, how does it make you feel? Less than? Silenced more?

I do feel immensely grateful that more young women today are finding their voices and paving the way for this knowledge to be much more available – as long as you have access to the internet you have access to knowledge.

Although not all internet access is good access. The use of porn is extremely damaging not only to boys, but also to girls/women. There has been a study conducted about the use of porn and its users. 51% of porn watchers are women. The average age of boy addicted to porn is 14, for a girl it's around 13.

The lower age in girls, I believe comes from a lack of knowledge about their bodies and a pressure to fit in, to feel sexy, and to see what is expected of them. With the easy access to porn and social media girls are left confused, intrigued, and wanting to have answers about their bodies. Why they don't fit in, and why does their body look so different to the porn stars or social media influencers.

Girls are interested in their bodies, what they should look like, smell like, feel like. How to be with another person, how to do sex acts to please another person. They get trapped into a cycle of their bodies aren't got their pleasure, but instead they should have sex for the pleasure of the man. This is what porn is teaching young girls and women. How to be an object of desire for someone else's gratification. Porn doesn't teach girls that they can say no, that they can ask for what they want, for them to be loved, appreciated, adored, loved, worshipped. Instead, it teaches disconnect from oneself. It teaches girls to be quiet and to just do what the man wants.

Porn and social media replaced the connections that women once had with each other and their partners. Over the generations of being told 'it's not lady like' or 'it's dirty and disgusting' to speak about sex and periods – which may I add it is 100% lady like, it is one of the most lady like things I could ever think of!

Ladies bleed. Ladies have an organ filled with thousands of nerve endings with no other job than to provide us with orgasms. It's pretty damn lady like to me.

"Ladies have an organ filled with thousands of nerve endings with no other job than to provide us with orgasms."

I want you to think back to a time when you have been told 'it's not lady like' to discuss those topics. Now you've heard just how lady like they are, imagine having a conversation with the person that told you not to. I want you to laugh and tell them *'it is lady like. It is what we are designed for, and I will speak my truth'*.
Do you feel scared saying it? Journal on it.
Maybe in your head you're having that conversation with your mum, or a grandmother or aunt. Can you see how much society had conditioned you not to see how womanly these things are and how terrifying it is as a woman to speak up about it to another woman. Even the conversations in our own minds can lead us to sweaty palms and not even want to do it. Even though the conversation isn't even real.
This is how society has kept us silent for so long.
This is how society has caused girls to look for the answers in dark places.
By keeping the older generations terrified of judgement, ridiculed, and separated it's caused them not share, or even hold any of the knowledge our ancestors held about the feminine. This is part of the witches wound. A wound all women still carry to this day, a wound I am working hard to heal not only for myself but for the women that came before me and the women that came after me. When we can be aware of how we have been silenced, shamed, punished. Then we can begin to find our voices, find peace within, and no longer feel punished for being a woman.
We carry this energy into our businesses, scared to speak, scared we will upset someone with our truth, with our light, with our knowledge. We struggle to find the right words, to come across confident, to capture ourselves on video or audios. Being scared to speak can lose you hundreds, thousands, millions. You are leaving so much on the table by fearing your own voice.

Have you ever had a deep soul filling conversation with your mother, grandmother, daughter, aunt, niece about periods, sex or money?

Not the conversations about using pads or tampons. Keeping clean and keeping those private things to yourself.

Not the conversations of spend some save some.

But the type of conversation telling you how powerful the womb portal is. How your menstrual blood is powerful? How to enjoy sex and relax into orgasms? How to make your money work for you, not you work for your money? How you get to decide how much income you desire, not what the boss tells you, you are worth?

How you are a creatrix and incredible manifestors. Did they tell you all about using your cycle to move and flow and feel everything life has to offer you? Did you talk about the magic that gets activated when becoming a woman? Did you talk about how to love yourself during the bleed and how we sync up with the moon cycles and other women around us? Did you talk about becoming the breadwinner in the family home? Did you talk about enjoying your money? Did you talk about becoming your own boss and working 10 hour weeks?

No?

Me either, I never had these conversations.

These were not available to my grandmother to pass onto my mother for her to pass onto me.

These are the conversations men did not want us to have and women didn't feel comfortable to have. These are the conversations that remind women we are the divine feminine and we are the creators of life and death. That we are powerful. When the collective knows and understand just how powerful they are, they can take back the world. Yet we are left divided, in as many ways as possible. Because when we are divided by the smallest of thing, we aren't powerful sisterhoods united against one enemy. Instead, we fight against each other.

We have been taught to hate that woman/girl who speaks openly about periods/sex. If she does that then she must be a slut. Sluts are horrible women and should be shamed for their actions.

If a woman is quiet and doesn't speak about sex/periods, then she is frigid and shy, and no man will love her because she will not give him what he desires.

We have been taught to hate that poor girl who lives in old clothes and to avoid her, not to be associated with 'those types of people'. We've been taught that the girls with money are stuck up bitches who got their money off their dads and never worked a day in their lives.

What keeps you divided from other women? What lies have you been told as a child to keep you imprisoned and separated from other women? What were you told about poor women, rich women and the women in-between?

There are countless names and phrases we have been taught on how to keep ourselves divided. Every generation has a different type of woman to hate against. The fat ones, the skinny ones, the loud and bold ones to the shy and quiet ones. The white ones, the coloured ones – I hate this one the most. Race has torn us up and divided us for far too long. We are all one race. The human race. We have been torn and stripped apart so we can never know our strength.

But I encourage you all, to learn and speak up. Even if your voice only reaches one woman, you could still change the lives of thousands of women through that one.

We have been torn
and stripped apart so
we can never know
our strength

I now have these conversations with my loved ones, my mother and grandmother, my foster children and social workers, other foster carers and clients and I will continue to speak this truth to as many men and women that I come across. I speak to my sons about the power of a woman, I show them how I step into my power and emotions being a woman, so I can lead them to grow up with their voices and the ability to show men and women how to find their voice and use it, with support empowerment and courage.

The most important person I speak to on all of my womanly attributes is my husband. I have been so badly hurt at the hands of men in my past, that me discussing with him anything intimate about myself brings forth a whole new level of healing every time. The more I am learning about myself, my cycles, my business, my limitations and beliefs I share with him. Not only so he knows when we are about to get our freak on and when to just give me space and feed me chocolate from afar. But as I teach my husband about what it is like to be married to a woman, a boss, a home maker, a care giver, a not taking your shit bad ass! He too is learning, he must learn that I am not his slave placed on this earth for his pleasure, a lot of men believe when they get with a woman she is to take over the role of his mother.

– Dear men, Fuck off. We are not your slaves nor do we ever wish to become one.

This is something I now like to tell my husband, but it was different when we first got together. I was scared and trapped in the old roles' society had created for us. I hated it. I was ready to give up on my relationship. Until I began to heal and remember I have a voice. I didn't have to live my life running around cleaning after everyone else. Sometimes as mothers we believe we do, we believe that's what a 'good mother/wife' does. But it's bullshit, and I'm calling it out. It lack of boundaries, self-respect and keeps far to many women from ever chasing their dreams.

If you are sick of cleaning up and being a slave to capable people around you, use your voice. Now that doesn't mean run around screaming telling everyone to fuck off, but you could call up a cleaning agency and get someone booked in twice a month to help you, or create a tasks board with little gold stars for people in the family to do. Set the rules you want for your home. You are the one not using your voice and getting annoyed because no one is listening. How can they listen when you aren't speaking up for yourself?

This goes for your business to, if you have a VA/PA and they are taking you for a ride but you won't say anything to them, that's on you. If you have clients who are demanding and rude and you allow them to speak to you in that way, that's on you.

You don't have to be rude when using your voice, but you have the permission right now to speak up about what you want.

Here's **Your Voices Permission Slip**. Not that you need it, but here you go! Take it. Run with it. Go forth and claim all that you desire.

Going back to my husband, I teach him about living with me so can teach our sons the role of a man/masculine in a relationship. The role of the man is not to simply go out to work, demand dinner on the table and sex as and when he places.

The role of the man in a relationship to lift and encourage and support his partner. It is to live side by side, with compassion, empathy, and space to feel loved and to give love.

But over the years as we have been cut off from our powers and so scared to speak out, we even get scared about speaking to our sons about the importance of their roles in life, regardless of if they are straight or gay. The same rules apply.

Our inner wisdom has been silenced for so long, we have no idea who we are or what we are, and if anyone does try to remind us, they are shamed. Called crazy, told it's all just woo-woo, and try to get taken down. It's the same principle in business, we need to understand the roles of the masculine and the feminine, and how they work together. How we can best utilize the change of energy through our cycles and sex. How and when to step into our masculine energy and when to step into our flow of feminine energy. By seeing what they look like externally in our environment we can start to see how those pieces fit into our business and how we can lean into those at the right time.

We've looked a lot into the feminine, but what does it actually mean to be in the masculine and how are we using our voices to cripple the masculine within ourselves and others around us. When you think of masculine what comes to mind?

A hench bloke, down the pub, lads, lads, ladsssss! – sorry if you know, you know.

Basically, a guy who is emotionless, tough, fights, and gets drunk. That's how masculinity has been pushed onto so many of us, that's the image of 'a manly man' here in the UK. That could be a different image for you, depending on where you are from, or live.

Journal what you believe is masculine, what does it look like to you, what does it feel like to you? Is it distant relationships, aggression, anger, lack of communication?

Or is it safety, emotions, warmth, support?

Whatever it is for you, write it out, draw it. See it. Then break it down. Is it the idea of masculine that you desire for yourself and within a partner. Notice how you are showing up as the tough emotionless person in your life, is it with your kids or husband? Are you showing up that way in business? Are you pushing through consistently, never giving yourself a break? Trying to prove your worth with emotion?

For me, becoming a mum to two gorgeous boys changed how I view men. My eldest son who is 11 as I write this book came to me when I knew no better. When I was only 18, I was in an abusive relationship with someone when he was 1 until 2. But that guy was an emotionless, aggressive, drunk. But he had good looks and worked out, exactly what I thought a 'man' should be. But my parenting was that of 'boys don't cry' 'toughen up' 'stop being a baby'. I never realised just how much this impacted my son, who was a soft, gentle, kind, emotional boy. When I got with my husband he wasn't my usual 'man' type, but he was the perfect masculine for my healing to take place. He taught me what masculine looked like, and that's a whole lot of tears, don't get me wrong he often struggles with the communication side of things but the more I learnt, the more he learnt and the more we could become better parents to our son. My 4 year old is allowed to cry and held when he cries, we ask him what's making him sad, where he feels the sad in his body, what it looks like to him, what colour shape ect. This is the easiest way for people to describe their feelings. My 4 year old might not say he is angry because of XYZ, but he will tell me his heart is a red hard square. Which I know to be he is angry at something, and we work with him to change the colours back to a neutral calm colour and then he goes about his day in a better mood. Whereas I'd shout at my son for crying and demand he stopped, because that's what I heard from my parents. I wasn't taught true masculinity when I had my first son, I had a lot of making up to do with him, to help him heal from the shit I caused. I now tell him to cry when he gets emotional, I hold him when he is upset, I encourage him to speak to me about how he is feeling and about his day. Even just being able to speak about the small things, he knows I am always available for the big things. He knows there will be no judgement, only love and support for his choices. Looking back I never would have known how to give him his voice. I was conditioned to silence, and I began to condition him to it too. Now I encourage him to speak as often as possible, but also on social media too so he can support others. He goes live on tiktok and speaks positivity whilst playing his games and chatting with friends.

My job is not only to raise the feminine energy, but to raise the masculine inline with the feminine, both in men and within women.

The masculine is all about being a safe place and supportive, providing for others and inner strength. Attributes that both men and when have, but in equal doses we shift our lives and the lives of other around us. When our sons cry, they are not weak for having emotions, but at that time they need someone else to take on the role of safety and comfort and hold them. Just like women need to feel safe and held when emotional, men too deserve the same. Unity. Balance. Ying Yang. Harmony.

Where do you feel like you need to be held?
Where do you feel like you need to do the holding?

It is not wrong to need nor give support and safety to another, especially to a son, partner, brother, cousin.
Men's mental health is at an all-time low, I believe as we raise our energy within both masculine and feminine, we can pave the way for men to see they too are safe to be human beings, feeling and experiencing life.

Just like women need to feel safe and held when emotional, men too deserve the same.

Speaking from the body

Our voice is connected to the pussy, in more ways than expected. If you ever get to see the images of a throat and pussy together you will be blown away – there is a picture on my Instagram if you are bursting to go see it follow me @jess.smithers.jones
So when our voice is silenced it also disconnects us from our powerhouse, our Goddess. It creates misalignment between our chakra's, which can make us feel really off balance in life. Like things just don't line up for us.

Shouting out loud just using your throat sounds totally different then when you clench your Kegel muscle and shout! I find it makes you sound louder without any extra force from the throat. Not only is shouting more fun when you have this connection but also orgasms are so much more fun.
Using breath work, moaning and pulsation of the pussy combined sets the body up for deep explosive orgasms that fill the whole body with life force energy.

There are many different breath techniques you can do. My favourite is a reiki breathing technique where you breathe in and on the exhale you clench your pussy and place your tongue on the roof of your mouth. You can feel the energy trap within your body, do this 5 times then on the 6th time you don't clench nor put your tongue on the roof on the mouth. Instead allow your body to let out all the energy and breath with a big, long moan. It feels delicious to do.

Masturbation Tips – Wanking with intention

Taking some well-deserved 'me' time is very important, and unless you are 100% comfortable trying new things with a partner, then I highly recommend doing this alone for a while, as getting into the rhythm is key.

I love to just lay down, I call it the pillow princess pose – but just get your naked self into any position that you feel comfortable in.

– Just to note there will be no porn access during this masturbation sessions. If your first reaction is 'oh fuck' then girl, you seriously need to detox off the porn.

No cheating. No porn.

In your comfortable position, begin to feel into your body, touching yourself - other than just your clit. Allow yourself to really feel your body, get to know what you like. Soft, rough, fast, slow. Take some time exploring.

Using your breathe take some long slow breaths in and out, and notice how that feels, allow your body to moan as and when you feel called to. You don't have to start off screaming 'ohh yes, ohh yes' because we know it's mostly just for our partners. But allow your throat to open as you moan into the touch.

Then when you feel ready to, go down to your pussy and allow her to feel the pleasure. Her job is to give you pleasure, so feel into that, allow your body to feel alive, to welcome and receive the pleasure that you are made for, deserving of, need!

Allow your body to moan as you breathe and feel. The point of this exercise isn't to get you to cum quickly, but for your body to feel fueled and soaked up in the pleasure. Notice how your moan sounds, notice how being on your pussy feels. Keep breathing long and slow breaths in and out as you feel your pussy purring in your throat. If you wish to allow your body to cum, keep going and allow yourself to moan through the orgasm, don't hold your breath either, if you continue to breathe through your orgasm, it allows the blood to move around the body causing you to feel your orgasm throughout your body and you're able to feel this from 10 seconds up to 2 minutes depending on how often you practice.

It's important you allow yourself to moan at what feels good, when you are able to moan during your own pleasure time, it can give you the confidence to ask for more of what do you want when it comes time for you to try this with a partner.

Being able to speak up about what you want from sex, helps you to find your voice in all other areas of your life, including your business.

Women living quietly, also equals to women living in poverty. Our silence around sex and periods also spilled over into our finances.

When you're silent about feminine energy, you will be silenced on masculine energy too.

Everything in life is energy, and everything in life is either feminine or masculine, Ying Yang. When you are silenced, you are fearful, when you are fearful you don't fulfil your goals and desires – because you have to speak over them.

When you speak over your goals and desires you add fuel to the manifestation, words are powerful. SPELLING, using words to create meaning or have a result. By using your words, you are creating spells, magick, miracles.

Your words hold so much power, the words you have on repeat in your mind, and the actual words you say out loud. Connecting to your words help you to reconnect to your power. This is why you have been forced to stay quiet for so long, this is what they don't want you to find out. This is why they keep us divide, busy in gossip rather than coming together and binding our spells in deep connection.

Your words are needed in all areas of life, if you look at how you write in your business does it capture your audience? Do you use your words to create a scene, to sell a story? Do you find that you can easily communicate your message with your clients? Are you able to voice your boundaries in business?

When you're silent about feminine energy, you will be silenced on masculine energy too

MANIFESTING QUEENS

Manifesting Queen of .... (insert your own)

I was introduced to the book The Secret at the age of 19, at that time I figured I would read a little bit and give it a whirl. I had nothing left to lose. Literally. I had no job; my flat was inhabitable, and I had a 3-month-old baby with no partner. I was living back at my mums and I needed a way out. So, I skimmed over the book and it said something about when you can see it, you can have it. I figured I would try it out with a house. I really wanted to find a house, my flat had no boiler, and was on the 3rd floor with no parking. I was sick of getting parking tickets every time I tried to take my shopping from the car and up to the flat. I wanted something big enough for me and my son to be safe and settled in. I tried to imagine what the house would look like, the beautiful open plan kitchen dinner, the lounge, large stairs, large bedroom for me and a good size room for my boy, I even added in a closet room. I wasn't overly fussed for a back garden, but parking was a must.

I sat with this image for 2 days, I had no deposit for a new place, but I just kept holding the idea that we would be moving into this house. I would see us dancing in the kitchen as he got older and playing in the lounge. I could hear him laughing away. Then on the evening of the second day I was scrolling through Facebook and someone had tagged me on a post for a 3-bedroom house. I still didn't have the money, but I messaged the lady straight away, and she agreed to let me view the property. My mum was going to come with me but was waiting on guests to arrive, so I took my grandad, and as soon as I walked into the place it was exactly how I had saw it in my mind, except the stairs were on the other side of the house than in my head, other than that it was perfect. My grandad offered the lady the deposit then and there and 1 month's rent. He also told me it was a gift, and I didn't have to pay him back. I was so shocked; I knew I was supposed to move into that house. I didn't know why; I just knew I was supposed to live there. It was the start of something beautiful, that was my first ever conscious experience of manifesting. From that house I manifested other things, things that even still to this day blow my mind and make me feel insanely happy and fascinated. I was driving back to the house one day with my boy in the car, a Blue VW Golf GTI that I'd also manifested. I had been asking for some cash as I needed to get a new fridge. I asked the universe once then forgot about it, as I began looking for work and assumed that I would get the money by getting a job.

On that day driving home I saw £20 on the floor, so stopped the car in the middle of the road, thankfully it was a quiet street. I got out to pick it up, but as I looked up I saw more £20's and £10's all across the road.

I picked it all up and got into the car, my hands were shaking and my heart beating insanely fast. I looked around but couldn't see anyone. I sat in the car for a few minutes but still no one showed up. I drove down to my house, put the money into my bag, got my boy out of his car seat and got into the house as fast as I could. I kept looking out the window but still there was no-one there. I counted the money and I had £200 exactly. The fridge I wanted was £190 I had the money for the fridge and a little extra. I couldn't believe it, still to this day I can't believe it. But I got my fridge, and I loved it.

These were some of my first big experiences of manifesting, but things weren't always that easy. Things happened to me along the way and life felt really hard. It didn't seem to matter how many times I read The Secret and did the same practicing as I had done previously. Things just felt hard. Relationships began to fall apart, I began to rack up debt, and I even found myself in an abusive relationship. I was Queen of the world for short periods of time but mostly I was scrapping by. I found this became my normal for a while. Dragging myself through to the next pay day. I had the house but my life inside that house became a mess.

The guy I was dating moved in pretty quickly, and it didn't take long before his drug addiction was taking over, he had his own past issues that have never been dealt with, and the anger was explosive. I did give back as much as I got, the anger building up inside me as my past caused us to fight like thunder and lighting. Trying to claim the dark sky as our own. I did things I'm not proud of and I said things I am not proud of, but I had to experience that version of myself. I had to embody the chaos and the anger to push me to the next level of myself.

There is an energetic level that we all live in.

"I had to embody the chaos and the anger"

I had to go through that pain and suffering so I could know what it felt like. It's a part of life. Yes, we have the capabilities to manifest, but our powers are still deeply connected to the lessons we need to learn to level up and our vibration.

Some people never level up, as they get so caught up in the drama rather than the lesson.

With every completed lesson we raise our vibration. When we raise our vibration, we make space for new opportunities to flood into our lives. It took me a while to realise this. When we live in the vibration of anger, shame, guilt the chances of getting those large amounts of money are so slim, because you aren't energetically aligned to large sums of money. Money carries its own vibration. That's why the saying rich people get richer, and the poor people get poorer is so true. Rich people are living at a higher level of vibration. Lack and scarcity aren't on their level, abundance and fun is their standard level of vibration. Yes, they have their own dramas at that level, but they are able to over come them and keep raising their vibrations. Poor people live in lack and scarcity, attracting more situations that amplify that experience and vibration.

For me, when I was living in that space of low vibrations, I hated everything. I hated the way I looked, I had a drug and drink problem, I hated the person looking back at me in the mirror. I grew to hate the man I slept next to at night. I hated my ex, who had moved in with his girlfriend across the road from me. I hated everything about my life.

I got more than one way out. Everything that needs to crumble will fall, to make space for the new to arise.

I had no idea back then that She was in control. I had stopped listening to her for a very long time. She made moves I never expected.

My ex who lived across the road with his new girlfriend, well it turned out he wasn't my son's dad. After a lengthily court battle for custody, my solicitor suggested a DNA test to delay proceedings.

A week later the latter came through my letter box- NOT the biological birth father.

Those words slapped me across the face. I couldn't believe it, but She knew. She had been trying to get me away from him for years. I had never listened. Weeks before that letter, we had even planned on running away together, with my son. She had to end it. From that day I never heard off him again. I got some abuse and backlash off his family and friends, but none of it hurt as much as knowing I would never have him in my life again. The man I had loved/hated for years, just one day was gone. I couldn't grief for him, my son had no idea what was going. Luckily to this day he doesn't remember him, he has no memory of what happened. But I have to live with it, all the time. It was hard, but I've healed from it now, now I can speak about it with ease, compassion and love for the chaos that was my life.

My then boyfriend lashed out at me and we got into a huge fight, and I decided to leave him to. It was enough to push me to take a job on a yacht abroad. I thought about taking him back, but then found out he had got someone else pregnant before I had left. He had been cheating on me for several months and she was due any time soon. The fight apparently happened because he was scared to tell me he had gotten her pregnant whilst we were trying desperately for a child. I had not even come close to conceiving a child with him. *She* knew. She knew he wasn't the right one for me. She had my back the whole time.

I had to go through the pain of losing two men out of my life to be able to rise to another level. The people in our lives are a huge factor to whether we rise up and create a different life or do we continue to keep learning the same lessons year after year without listening and learning, without progression and without up leveling our abilities to manifest new ways of being.

Manifesting is just the word used to say – **bringing in new things at my vibrational state of awareness**.

When you understand where you are on the vibration scale you can see the levels of work and self-awareness needed to reach the next level to be able to bring in more. Manifesting is a beautiful process when we tap in and use our vibrations (and vibrators).

Since I have learnt this process more things have fallen into place than they ever did in the 10 years previously, that includes the time of the house and money on the floor.

When I got into sync with myself this book emerged, after years of on and off trying. I've generated £5k months as a minimum.

I have attracted the perfect mentor in my life to support me and encourage me. From amazing photos that I was so beautifully guided to create, to the perfect website system, to the best branding and all the creative ideas to build my business.

I listened to my body and my energy, and I watched the magic unfold.

So much pressure is on people to just know and be able to manifest £20k months, but that is really hard when you're earning a wage or on a low income. It feels like too much of a stretch and it then becomes unavailable to you in your current vibration as it fills you with fear and lack. Forcing yourself to be at a higher vibration is unsustainable and also very fake.

It's not a case of fake it until you make it, rather break it down to build it up, to make it. Like a house, you don't fake having a house and one day it just appears, but instead foundations need to be laid, bricks set, walls made, and everything else that goes into building a house. It's the process of building the house that the fun and magic lays in, not just opening your eyes one day in the hopes that it will be made over night whilst you slept.

Manifesting is so hyped up, but we manifest all day every day. That's right, even the shit stuff. Because energy and vibration don't give a crap whether you are putting out high or low energy, all they do is return to you what you give out. So, if you are still riding in that low energy and experiencing one bad thing after the next. Pause. Breathe. Evaluate.

The stuff coming into your energy regardless of if it's from other people is still a reflection of what you are putting out. If you find yourself caught up in the drama, but still going to the shop every Friday to put a lucky dip on, odds are you aren't going to hit the jackpot. It's just not energetically aligned to you.

Becoming aware of what you are manifesting is so important, this awareness can also be found when you tap into the juicy knowledge of your periods. They aren't just a struggle that women have to go through every month. They hold so much power and vibration, they can help you run your business when you learn how to use them to your benefit.

If you find yourself in the rat race of life, and trying to stay consistently on the go, pushing through, when all your body wants is a luxury hot bath and to curl up in a warm bed then I'm pretty sure you experience your month like an emotional and vibrational roller coaster.

One week you're smashing through everything with pure ease, the next thing whilst you are bleeding it feels as though you have the weight of the world on your shoulders, and you feel useless to everyone. Blaming your period, hating your period, feeling lesser than, to a man because of your bleed.

"Your months don't have to feel like a roller coaster"

Your months don't have to feel like a roller coaster, and you also don't have to experience that level of manifestation in your life either.

The times when you feel like you're on top of the world and good things are showing up, that's the level you can have even whilst you're on your period. I know for many it is going to be mind boggling to even think during your period things can go smoothly. I'm going to let you in on a secret to your period and to manifesting that is probably against everything you thought before.

No - to manifesting during your period OR under the new moon. Mic drop!

I know this is totally going to confuse a lot of you, but I encourage you to bare-with me and keep reading.

Your cycle isn't just your period, it's broken down into four phases just like the moon. Your period isn't the beginning of the cycle it is the end, just like the new moon. They are the end of the cycle. Their energy is all about releasing and letting go. I know many people these days are telling people to go out and manifest under the new moon. Every time you are doing that you are releasing all that you no longer want. So, if during the new moon you are seeking large financial growth, it won't come.

Also, for a lot of women our cycles sync up to the moon's cycles. Even if you don't actually bleed, your body naturally follows the moon's cycle.

So, if you are bleeding and trying to manifest under the new moon energy you are doubly letting it all go. So those things you are really wanting to call into your life won't be on their way any time soon, also your vibration is much lower at this time. It's thanks to the hormone change in your body when self-doubt, self-worth, self-love is at their lowest unless acted upon. This action happens at the beginning of the cycle.

Forcing yourself at your lowest point to try and feel better just doesn't work, you just end up putting more pressure on yourself causing you to fall back down the vibration chart, which means you then actively are trying to manifest from that lower vibration. Causing you to have the same experiences month after month. – The roller coaster periods.

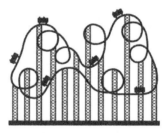

Knowing that trying to manifest under the new moon and being on our periods in facts lowers our vibration then we need to find the right time to create our new energetic minimum to create a stairs effect of vibration.

Learning how to hold this vibration through your monthly cycle isn't difficult but taking note of where you are is important. Journaling or using the free PDF at curvyco.uk/freebie is a great way to help you understand your cycle and manifesting. Hundreds of years ago it would have been normal for villages to bleed together and manifest together for the benefit of the village. Over hundreds of years this knowledge was lost, but I'm on a mission to bring it back. By hosting One Red Tent Retreat event a year. More detail can be found at curvyco.uk
Through the knowledge left to us, when we seek, we shall find.

This energetic minimum is how the rich stay rich, and the poor stay poor. For the poor their steps are a steep way down. For the rich they expect without doubt that more is coming. Not only financially but also in life and business. They are not only rich with wealth, but they live and experience life totally different to a poor person. They expect to have amazing things in their lives, the lush holidays, meals, experiences. Whereas a broke person finds lack and fault in every area of their life. The more lack and fault you find in your life and business, the more the universe will give you.

OHH SHIT, IT'S TABOO

Sex & Money. We *NEED* it.

"Money = Sex.
When it comes to having sex or making money, you're supposed
to know what you're doing and be all great at it, but nobody
teaches you anything about it. You're not supposed to talk about
it because it's inappropriate, dirty, and not so classy.
Both money and sex can provide unthinkable pleasures, birth new
life, and inspire violence and divorce. We're ashamed if we don't
have it, we're even more ashamed to admit we want it, and we
will do things/people we're not nuts about in order to get it."
-Jen Sincero

When I first shared my journey about coaching about sex and money/business I was worried how I would be viewed, but a friend of mine sent me this quote. She too, has an incredible online business, and understands the importance of sex and money. When I read this statement, it summed up perfectly what I knew to be true. It's all the subjects we're not allowed to talk about, but so desperately want to scream about.

What if we changed all of that? What if we no longer felt fear, shame, judgement when we spoke about these 3 things.
To not feel shamed when you say 'I just had the best sex of my life' or 'I'm bleeding like crazy' or even 'I just made £70k this month!'.
How freeing would it be to know that you can shine just for simply being you?!

 Sex plays a huge part in how we view ourselves but also the world around us. Sex additions or celibacy. Whore or virgin. Casual sex or long-term relationships. Ourselves or others.
All of it teaches us something about ourselves, even if we don't want to listen at that time, there will come a time in our lives where we do look at our sexual patterns and get to work on them. For me, sex is a large part of who I am.
What I stand for, and what drives me in life. I don't have a conventional sex life. It's been crazy but I wouldn't have it any other way. I shared with you how disconnected I was at my first sexual experience, and that disconnect continued for years. I now know the cause of my disconnect and it stems from my childhood and my relationship with my parents growing up. My mum and brother were very close, and my dad worked away and when he was home, he wasn't present. I was desperate to feel loved, to be accepted, to be wanted by someone.

There stems my bad relationship with sex. Now I'm not blaming anyone for my actions, my actions were based on how I felt, and what needs weren't met, but ultimately, I had the decision and power to act or not to act. At the time it was just easy to blame others and act out.

Not everyone with a bad relationship with sex was sexually abused, so I encourage you to look at your childhood and see if there was something that happened there that caused you not to feel loved enough, good enough, or wanted.

If you were sexually abused as a child, know that none of it was your fault, and I send you the biggest hug.

In my personal life I am surrounded by countless people, young and old, that have been victims to sexual abuse at a young age. It is far more common than most people realise.

Your experience is unique to you, but please don't feel alone. Reach out, you might be surprised at other people's stories too. Being sexually abused as a young girl or experiencing lack of emotional stability from parents can cause your inner Goddess to be shut off from you, making it harder to connect to yourself spiritually but also not being able to understand that aspect of yourself. If there is this disconnect, chances are your first bleed experience wasn't a celebration to welcome you into woman hood either.

Let's normalize these types of tough conversations too. Good sexual encounters. Bad sexual encounters. Talk about them, share your message. It's what's shaped you to be who you are today.

I was spiked and stripped naked and abused during my time in Spain working on the yacht. It was the reason why I gave up my job and came back to the UK. I don't have much memory from that night. I remember a security guard was doing his round of the docks and found me in a doorway. He put his jacket on and took me inside the security gates to where the boat I was working on was. Luckily he has seen me leave my boat earlier that night and got me onto the boat. He placed me inside and called for the captain. I woke up in so much pain and so embarrassed, I spent the next day in a&e in a hooked up to IV drips and on loads of medication to ensure I didn't contract HIV or any other sexually transmitted disease. I felt so ashamed, I felt sick that it happened to me. I was angry with myself, I was angry with the world. I had gone out with 2 other people off the boat and I said I was just going to stay and finish my drink and I'd catch them up. I never did catch them up. When I got home from the hospital the chef had made me some food and a hot drink. The guys I went out with didn't speak to me much, but I could tell they felt awful.

The next morning I still didn't feel amazing but I spoke to my mum back home and cried. I wanted to go home. So I decided to leave working on the yacht and head back home.

I didn't give myself time to deal with it, I pushed through and pretending like nothing happened. When friends asked why I went back home I would lie, or blame different things.

In all honestly, I was more ashamed and embarrassed than anything else.

I got sucked straight back into my old ways with relationships and sex. If anything I found it much harder than ever before. I couldn't look at the person I was sleeping with and I kicked them out even faster than before. I was numb to sex. I became numb to life.

"Normalize these types of tough conversations"

Where do we get to the point in life where sex isn't such a horrible subject and it's also not a subject dripped in fairy dust. Sex is so powerful, even if you aren't into sex spiritually, it's still damn powerful and has the ability to make you do stupid and amazing things.

Sex & money is everything. Just like the feminine and masculine. They can be seen and portraited in any light.

I know what it's like to have conversations with women about sex, but also with men. Being in the Army for 6 years did come with it's benefits at times.

I know how differently women feel and experience sex, not only physically but emotionally too.

Men have a different view on sex. Depending on the man, a different outcome or expectation of the sex.

I wish more people could have more honest and open conversations about sex, for sexual partners to have conversations about their sex. To feel safe enough to discuss what it is they experience during sex and what they would like to experience. This may become the conversation that ends that relationship – and that's okay!

Because life is too short to be having shit sex, with no connection! It may become the conversation that deepens the relationship and takes the connection to a whole new level of openness and awareness to each other.

Chatting to your friends about your sex life might feel easy and free, to have a space to moan and complain about the sex or to soak in all the bliss it brings, but to turn and sit with your partner might feel terrifying. I know I've been there myself with my husband. I could easily sit and moan to my friends about how I felt after sex, but I could never bring myself to tell him. I was afraid I sounded needy or that he would think I was strange.

Then one day I decided nothing will change if he doesn't know there's a problem.

Que Mic Drop. Mind Exploding Situation.

Let me just repeat that for those in the back.

NOTHING WILL CHANGE IF HE DOESN'T KNOW THERE'S A PROBLEM.

Well, fuck me. How crazy did I feel?!

I had allowed a situation he wasn't even aware of to crush me for months hoping that it would change.

In all honesty, it wasn't even anything big, but the more it happened, the bigger it got for me.

The worse I felt, it caused me to not want to have sex with him just to avoid that feeling.

We do that in business too. Create a problem in our own minds that no one else may be aware of and yet we don't talk about our issue or we rip people's heads off when they ask if we are okay. We can stop ourselves from pushing to the next level, because of something very small, so small that if we shared it with a team member or business bestie they would be able to help us and fix our problem in less than 2 seconds.

So here is my big – nonexistent – problem.

I wanted to feel loved, after the sex had finished. I wanted to be hugged, kissed on the head, and held. I wanted to feel safe after sex.

I know, so small. But it was huge for me. We used to finish having sex, then he'd just snuggle under the sheets and say goodnight. I felt like a knife going through my heart. Granted this wasn't happening every time we had sex, but at least 80% of the time.

Remember back to when I said I had disconnected, one-night stands. Well, I've also slept with men for money. There was never any affection and as soon as it was done you would leave, or they would leave. I've kicked people out straight after having sex and I've been kicked straight out. I've had the sex where I've been used, and I've used others. With my husband, not feeling loved after sex, made me feel used, it made me feel like a prostitute without being paid. It made me feel like I was just there for his benefit – even if I'd had the best orgasm of my life. It was what happened at the end that triggered me so much.

So, I put my big girl knickers on, and I told him how I felt, I explained everything. We had a real, raw, honest conversation about sex. How it made me feel, and how I experienced it, and also how he felt and experienced it. He had no idea about my problem – because it was just that. My problem that I hadn't shared.

Now I never, ever have that problem, I shared it with him and he fixed it.

So many of us have these sex problems, they consume us, they cause us not to want sex, not to talk about sex. They cause us to feel shame and guilt and make us want to shrink into a dark hole. This is exactly why we need to break down the barriers, let go of thinking we can't openly talk about sex. Sex is the foundations of our relationship with our partners. Without sex, we just have friendships.

Just the same way sex makes us hide away and not want to face our problems, business can do the same. If you aren't feeling loved in the bedroom chances, are you hide back in your business or you try to chase the love in your business. Either way you never feel good enough or satisfied enough to keep pushing through or giving up.

"Without sex, we just have friendships."

SEX HAS A LOT TO ANSWER FOR

The more aware I become to the impact sex has had on my life, I realise it has impacted everyone's lives around me.

Sex is at the root of everything, even though we think money is. Your existence is due to your parents having sex, and they are here because of their parents, and you will go on to have kids, and so the cycle is.

But it's deeper than that. It's at the center of who we are as a person to.

Sex can be the root cause of immense trauma and abuse, and it can also be the root of all our pleasures and desires.

Wherever you are in life, sex will be having an impact on you. It's often the reason why people have affairs and get into debt, it's often the reason why people get into relationships, and it's often the reason why people leave relationships.

What does sex look like for you in your life? Where are you seeing your sex life impact you?

They might sound like unimportant questions, but the truth is, sex impacts everything.

Sex has been the reason I have got into so many stupid situations over the years. Sex had been the reason why I stayed in terrible relationships and left kind men. It was the reason why I left my job working on a private Yacht and the reason why I share this knowledge today.

The sex I have today is a totally different type of sex I had 10 years ago. The sex I was engaging in before left me feeling insane lack. I felt un-loved, un-lovable, un-worthy, disrespected, dirty, cheap, closed off.

Those emotions I was carrying around with me all the time, causing me to be bringing that into my everyday life. I worked in a hotel, that was minimum wage, long hours, I felt un-worthy, I felt not good enough, and my life was filled with so much drama. A constant treadmill of shit.

The more sex I would have with different men, in the hopes to feel loved, I was left feeling more of the same crap. I allowed them to treat me that way, as that was as that's how I felt about myself. My internal energy was being showed to me on the outside and I hated it. Yet I was stuck in a cycle of doing the same thing and getting the same crappy results. It's an easy cycle to get caught up in, especially when you have no idea what else to do to try and fill the emotion's you are lacking in.

I felt cheap, and I was broke, financially, physically I was worn out and cast aside.

I allowed my body to be used, just in the hopes that I would feel something, I would spend most of my wages on new outfits, alcohol, and drugs just in the hopes of finding some sort of emotional benefit on the weekend, in the form of a boyfriend to love me.

What does sex have to answer for in your life?

This part of the book I encourage you to pause for a moment, pick up a pen and grab your YPYB Journal. Take your time answering these questions and come back to them as often as you need. You may find every time you answer them something new comes up for you. The deeper you go on your journey, the more will come up to heal.

If you feel safe to do so, you can share any answers or ask your own questions in our private Facebook community – ***Sacred Women in Business – CurvyCo***

Get real with yourself, be honest and let what you need to out.

When you think of sex what is the first word that comes to mind?

How was your first sexual experience?

How was your last sexual experience?

How do you feel you have changed between these two times?

Do you feel connected during sex?

How do you want to feel during sex?

Do you feel seen, heard, and understood during sex?

Do you feel connected to yourself during sex, alone or with a partner?

What sexual traumas are you holding onto?

How comfortable are you speaking to a partner about your wants and desires?

Do you view sex and money as shameful?

Do you connect sex and money with prostitution/porn/onlyfans? – sex and money together are dirty.

Do you feel comfortable talking about your finances?

Do you hide your body?

Do you hide your finances?

Do you have sex in the dark?

Do you feel in the dark to your finances?

Do you feel like your life is juicy, orgasmic and basically have more good days than bad?

There's loads of questions to be asked about sex, money & business.

SEX AND BUSINESS

So where does the connection really come into play?

I'd say from the very beginning, even the planning phase it should be taken into consideration. Sex is more than just intercourse. Sex is the connection between masculine and feminine. But it affects every area of your business.

The business part of your life is your masculine energy the systems, the money, the strategy. The sex is your higher self, the divine feminine energy, the pleasure, the receptive motor, the creatrix.

Pussy calls in the money. The masculine takes the action to bring in the money.

For a long time, my pussy and I didn't get on, and even though money was always in my life and I had enough. It was always being called out of my life. There was always something making the money leave, an unexpected bill, things breaking. You name it, it was happening. Money just wasn't sticking around long enough for me to get the full pleasure of it.

The pleasure of having money and enjoying it is key to understanding how money stays in our lives and how we can bring more of it into the physical existence. Being open to having pleasure in all areas of our lives and being able to welcome pleasure in many forms is great way of noticing if your receptive motors are on or not.

Grab a pen and your YPYB Journal and answer these questions, but make sure you are as honest as you possibly can be.

How do I feel when I'm are given a complement?

How do I react?

Do I brush it off?

Do I try to give that person a complement back?

Do I feel uncomfortable and try to ignore it?

Do I fully own the complement?

Do I say thank you with grace and pleasure?

If you struggle to accept a complement, you will struggle to receive £5k a month. It's all energy. If you aren't open to some one's words which hold less of an active vibration in you, then you will struggle to receive their money. Today we hold money in such a high vibration that so many of us have put money on a pedestal, we feel it's out of our reach, on a different level.

Like that hot guy who you think is out of your league, you don't even try, you hold money to that same standard.

We've been told that money is a solid 10, and that we're a basic 2.

But that's where you're pussy and business get to collide and become a creative, abundance, money making machine.

Your connection to your pleasure, your visions during meditation and masturbation and finally the doing parts to allow the money to flow through to you.

You have two parts.

Pussy is your direct link to source, your creative idea's.

Business is the links, the images, the words, the payment systems.

Let's break it down and see what area isn't fully connected in your business then we can amend those area's so they can work in sync with each other.

Grab yourself a pen and your YPYB Journal and let's figure out where you are.

Don't forget you can share this in the – **_Sacred Women in Business_** Facebook Community

Pussy

- Daily Meditations – min 10 minutes
  Are you spending 10 minutes minimum sitting with your higher self? Asking her to use you as a vessel to create, for

idea's to flow through you so you can bring them into the physical.

- Dancing/Moving
Are you spending time in your body? Allowing your body to move, to realise any built-up stagnant energy trapped in the body.

- Masturbating/Self pleasure
Are you connected to what your body likes? Do you give yourself pleasure? Do you prioritize your body and her needs/wants/desires? Are you using that pleasure time to visualise your dream life?

- Yoni Steams
Are you connecting to your pussy with intention? Allowing yourself to be guided, knowing that she has the ability to bring forth all you desire, even if you aren't fully aware of all that is yet. Sitting with intention let's your pussy/higher self, know that she is important. You are infusing her with herbs, steam, love and reaffirming to the universe that you are important, your creativity is important, and you are worthy of all things beautiful and abundant. – If you're not down to steam yet, set the intentions in the bath.

Business

- Brand
  What/Who is your brand? What colours? Patterns? Vibes?
  Mission Statement?

- Payment systems
  How are you getting paid? Does it feel good getting paid
  that way? How many payment options do you have?

- Platforms
  What platforms are you using? Are you just using social
  media? Do you have a website? Email list? Facebook, IG,
  TikTok, YouTube, Snapchat?

- Graphics
  What are you using for your IG, Facebook posts, Stories?
  Freebies? Documents?

-

Where are the two working together?
Where do you feel aligned and disconnected?

It's your business to know your pussy and your business.
To know what she desires and what your business desires. To
know what makes her tick, and most of all, what gives her the
most pleasure in life. Just like it's your business to know what is
going on in your business, what products/services you are
launching next, what brings in cash flow and what payments plans

are working.

It could be the pleasure of deep connected sex, or it could be the pleasure of being CEO to her own company generating over 1 million a year.
It could be the pleasure of opening a dance school or having an orgasm a minimum of once a week.
It could be getting into the best physical shape of your life and competing at a body building show, or it could simply be using a yoni steam and spending 10 minutes a week surrendering to honoring her.
Knowing what your pussy needs is your business, understanding what she needs and how she looks. What she calls for in your life and what makes her feel uneasy.
We dismiss her. Ignore her calls. Not think she is important. Not even know what she sounds like. It's our business to know our selves, to know our bodies. But we aren't taught it at any point in our lives, it's only as we get older and realise - fuck what everyone thinks of me. That's when we get to learn more about ourselves, but that knowledge is available from the very beginning. You don't have to go years taking the shit, you can take control over yourself now. You can create that business you always wanted now. You can create that course you have always wanted to, sell those products that you love.
The key to success is more self-awareness. The more you are aware of yourself, the easier it becomes to allow money to flow into your life. For you to let go of everything that was ever holding you back.
No truly know yourself, is to find yourself.

The key to success is
more
self-awareness

CYCLE WEEKS

I count my cycle different to most people. Most people count your first day of bleeding as the first day in your cycle, but I personally believe it's the last part of your cycle. I've held this knowing for such a long time, and the more I began to share it the more other things were popping up for me to take notice of. I had never seen nor heard of the pagan wheel of the year until I began writing this book. The pagans believed the year begins in Spring, and celebrate their new year around April. This made so much sense to me, it was a holy shit this makes so much sense. Our bodies follow a seasonal path, from Spring to Winter. Our ancestors knew this, and lived in accordance to the seasons. Sowing seeds and harvesting, using the moon, building communities.

For you have had your first bleed, your body would have gone through the other parts of your cycle first, the spike in estrogen, the release of the egg, the drop in hormones and finally your first bleed. Your body had already begun its cycle before your bleed. So, your bleed is the last part of the cycle, not the first. Your cycle begins in the Spring/pre ovulation and ends in the Winter/menstruation. But you are free to count your cycle days how-ever it feels right for you, no pressure, as long as it feels good for you. The counting of the days isn't that important, but it's understanding your seasonal cycle that is. That's where you can access all the juicy knowledge, by knowing where you are at what time of the month and what that means for you and your business.

Starting off in the first week of your cycle. This is from the 1st day after your bleed. This phase is your Pre-Ovulation week/phase, this is where you will have a little shift in your estrogen as your body begins to prepare for ovulation. This is the best time to start planning, start setting up your meetings or client calls for the next two weeks. During this time, you will find conversations flow much easier, your ability to take things on board and get things done more efficiently. When I'm shifting though the end of week 1 and into week 2, time feels to slow down as I busy myself getting everything I need done, done. Time slows to allow me to push through, so I am prepared for the end of my cycle.

As your hormones begin to change your mindset shifts causing your vibration to change. This is key to being able to up level each cycle, as show with the stair's method. Meditation during this time may not feel like a priority because you will see everything that you need to get done, but if you spend just 10 minutes a day feeling into your higher-self, consciousness, universe, God. You will be able to hold that higher energy for longer throughout the month, by starting to hold this energy from the beginning of your cycle you will be able to keep the momentum going of high energy even when you are at the end of your cycle and you are shedding/bleeding. It's the stability of this energy that helps keep you level throughout the whole cycle instead of feeling the up and down roller coaster of emotions and energy. You may have days/time where you feel your emotions dip but due to the high vibrations already active in your vortex you are more likely to bounce back quicker and still be able to generate the outcomes you are seeking to manifest.

Week 1 is all about setting the tone for the rest of your cycle. Allowing yourself to come out of your bleed, to step into spring, to feel the warmth of sunlight on your skin, the bounce in your step, everything around you beginning to blossom and that sense of new live is all around you.
You feel better in yourself and looking at yourself in the mirror isn't as scary as it was the week prior as your body ached and you lived in your sweats.

Spring is literally the best springboard you need in your business and life. This is the time when you get the chance to plan, set meetings, book yourself for speaking engagements, whether that looks like doing a 3-day mini course on your social media or being a guest speaker on a podcast, start looking for opportunities, come your summer season you will be in full swing.
You can use this time to write down any goals you would like to achieve for the following month, allow yourself to sit into the energy of it.
Create the time and space in your life for meditation, it will help you with your goals.
You might find that your energy is spiking and sitting to meditate for a long time can be challenging, so set an alarm for just 10 minutes to allow yourself to feel into receptive energies.

The Pre-Ovulation phase is the time to call things in, it's time to be bold in your decisions to bring it in. Know that everything you have been asking for is yours and on its way.

Then get out of your own way. Know that it's a done deal and keep moving forward.

In business that is asking for the goal then living like its arrived. Using and harnessing the powers of the law of attraction.

Ask. Believe. Receive.

Pre-Ovulation is a great time to also add a yoni steam into your week. Clearing out the energies from your last bleed and detoxifying your body. It's a great time to sit with your yoni and drop down into that space with intention.

Your pussy is magical, and she holds your creative energy, when you sit with her with intention to create you bring her to life and allow the magic to flow through her to you.

Yoni steams are a Chinese medicine have been around for centuries, and I hope to encourage more women in the western world to take full advantage of the medicine these provide to our pussies.

If this is something you are interested in there's more information on ***curvyco.uk*** and you can also purchase your own set and gold gown off our website.

Your pre-ovulation is you stepping out from your feminine energy of the bleed into the masculine energy of productivity.

You're moving out of the being and into the doing. That doesn't mean you have to be 'doing' all the time. You are given time to ease into the big flow of doing, time to find your feet before you start running next week.

You're starting to be a bit more chill this week, things that got under your skin last week don't seem to bother you as much and you begin to feel the urge to have more fun.

I highly recommend dancing like a Goddess in the kitchen. The kitchen is a great place to do this as it's often referred to as the heart of the home. Open your heart up to fun, joy, laughter, spontaneous enjoyment. Turn up the music and feel the gratitude run through your body as you begin to move. Move your arms, your neck, your hips, your feet. Let your body be free to just move.

No judgement.
Just presence.

Notice how your body is so receptive to feeling good. It's so natural to feel good whilst your body is moving freely, letting go of all restrictions, all self-doubt, all limitations.

The cortisol will be flooding your blood system causing you to feel bliss, happiness, joy. It also helps to keep you healthy and vibrant. Dancing like a Goddess helps to connect you into your feminine energy, to touch your body sensually, to move your birthing hips, to connect to your inner slut. We all have one, go on, let her come forward and play with her energy. She is naughty and seductive, she wants to be seen, to be touched, to be played with. She is that sparkle in your eye, the lust in your heart.

Dance with her, and watch how your day, week unfolds.

When you dance with her, you allow her energy to come to the surface, and she loves to play. Her energy is full of desire and pleasure. She will bring you more of that, more desires, more pleasures, because it all feels just so damn good to her.

Now you've began to wake her up, listen to what she is wanting.

Is she wanting you to create something new?

Is she wanting to be close to your partner?

Is she wanting to be intimate with you?

Open your heart up
to fun, joy, laughter,
spontaneous
enjoyment.

For me during the first 3 days of my spring season I still feel the energies from the previous bleed, so my body is in a place of wanting comfort but with a bit of adventure. Like waking from a long winters sleep, I want to explore the outside world, but the nights are still cold, so I still want that comfort at the end of the day. I love spending time with my partner during this time, early nights, walking the dog, breakfast in the city (if he is off work). I feel deep immense gratitude during this time of my cycle, and I love that I can just look at him and my body gets flooded with gratitude, love, abundance. These energies fill me up, they make me want to just be more present but also excite me to see what the universe is going to match up for me in that energetic space. Sometimes it's finding the perfect parking spot or grabbing the last table in a café. Finding £30 in an old coat pocket I've not worn in ages or signing a new client that day.

Use your pre-ovulation phase to tap into those emotions, you're setting the energetic minimum for your new cycle, you can either use it or end up back on the rollercoaster of emotional chaos.

I missed out on years' worth of this valuable knowledge whilst being on contraception for roughly 14 years, only coming off to have both my boys and my baby I lost.
I had no idea that this knowledge and a different way of living was available and naturally mine. I had a IUD fitted for the best part of those 14 years, I tried the pill and the injection but settled with the coil due to not remembering to take the others, I was told the IUD was my best option with 5 years of not being able to get pregnant – they also didn't tell me during this time I would have a dull flat-line experience of life.
I talked about this on one of my Master Classes, which was

amazing to share my experience of how I felt like I was flat lining, but I wasn't the only one who felt like that. Having an IUD or being on other forms of contraception for long periods of time causes us to go into a zombie like mode. I had no experience of feeling the summer sun on my skin as my energy began to spike in my natural spring state, I didn't get to experience the insane thirst for my partner during my summer season. I didn't experience my ability to assess and evaluate myself and work, and I most certainly didn't get to feel the coming of winter, the shedding, the bleeding, the letting go. My life was a dull straight line of same shit different day, and it was causing me to hate my life. I wanted to run away. Like pack a bag and run. I hated my life, I hated my job, my partner, my kids, myself.

But when I had the IUD removed, it was as if someone lifted the blurry veil I had been living behind, and my life began to come into colour. I began to feel into life again. I began to experience my seasons I began to tap back into my natural state and ohh boy is it beautiful.

Not only have I noticed how different life feels, but even my incredibly patient husband has noticed the difference in me. He is starting to understand who I am more and what I am bringing to the relationship but also to the family home. His position of being in the masculine has shifted to, before I didn't feel like I needed to be held, kept safe and secure. But now when I move into my bleed, his touch is different, and I embrace it. I feel his warm chest on my cheek as I lay on him wrapped up in bed. Just breathing him in, noticing how safe I feel at that time. That my body is safe to be in her feminine because I am being held by his masculine. Not dominance, but his masculine, the father, the protector, the safety, the provider.

During my summer season it is totally different again, I want to dance around the kitchen with him, I want to run my fingers through his hair, I want to sing (all be it badly) I want to go on walks and talk about things that we can do together on his day off and I look for new places to go. Even if it is a new place to go for breakfast, this time of my cycle I want to be with him, I want to spend time with him doing things, I want to hold his hand and laugh as we walk down the cobbled streets of Chester City. It sounds so romantic as I type it out, but it isn't always that romantic but it's a time I cherish and look forward to. It's the time where our relationship gets to feel like it's just the two of us again. This isn't always possible for every cycle so on the days when we can't, we love holding hands and eat pancakes for breakfast as I try to bring that energy back home.

I try to have early nights; we are in a good routine with the kids so that makes this time a lot easier for us to manage. The kids go to bed and we do to, but that doesn't mean lights out by 8pm. It's a time for us to shut the door on the world and just allow it to be the two of us. Our lives are so busy, but during this time of the cycle my body wants to be close with him. Not always intimately but just closer, but I usually can't keep my hands off him. I want to talk about nothing and everything. Goals, dreams, a funny joke I try to tell but end up just laughing at myself. The holding hands, the eye contact, the connection that allows me to be fully seen by him at that moment and know that I can be my truest self and still be loved, seen and valued.

That's the energy my body slips into, but check what your energy is calling out to you. All our cycles are personal to us, you may be crazy horny for a day or two or for 2 whole weeks, or you may notice you aren't getting what your body needs, and then you can start to take action to ask for what your body needs. If you are single, you can still apply this, notice what your body is calling out for, it could be found in doing something special for yourself, or taking yourself on a date or having a hot bath to allow you to relax into your energy. You can take that energy and focus it into your business.

As I mentioned earlier by starting out this cycle with meditation will help you to see where your energy is flowing to and from. You can begin to see something new that you want to implement in your business, it could be the idea's of launching a new course or selling a new product. It could be that you feel your business is ready to feel supported and you're ready to hire a VA or someone to create something for you.

The energy you feel into your cycle will help you to grow and flourish through your next cycle. It's the stepping-stone to development within your business and personal life. It's a great time to reach out to others and begin to watch the world unfold. Ask for the support if you feel you need it, if you don't feel ready during spring/summer time for support, ask yourself again during your autumn/winter season. Then the following cycle begin to look for someone during your spring phase so when you need to take a step back you already have someone there to help pick up what you need help with. Go back to Finding Your Voice if you feel you will struggle with giving someone directions/tasks.

For me, that person is my husband. When I first began to tap into the feeling and patterns of my flow, I didn't want any help, in fact I was pretty damn adamant, and my husband would probably use the words stubborn bitch. Who am I to argue with that, haha. I was loving my newfound superpowers, I felt like a ninja with a new weapon, doing summer saults across the floor in a power rangers' outfit. Now writing this I wish I actually had a power rangers costume – note to self, buy one. The pink one though.

I was ready to take on the world, all of my idea's and still run the house and keep 5 other people and a dog alive. I began to realise that even though I was capable of doing it all, when my body was ready to hide away and bleed, I didn't want to be wonder woman. But in my first 2 weeks of my cycle I was wonder woman, and I handled my shit very well. I was like a busy bee, doing everything whilst time slowed to allow me to get it all done, but I really needed help when I was in my bleed. I needed him to even help with the house and kids, not because my bleed time is bad, but because my body is tired, and needs softness.

You can track your cycle in your YPYB Journal. Notice how you feel during the different phases of your cycle. This will help you to see when you're more available and when you want to hide.
I have created a free Cycle Tracker Wheel for you to use in the back of your YPYB Journal. This will help you to see how you feel throughout your cycle and when you are Wonder Woman and when you need to hide away from the world.
If you feel that you can't step back from your business to bleed, journal where that limiting belief has come from. You're business flows with your energy, you can still receive clients and money when you take time for yourself.

Ask for the support
if you feel you
need it.

The Stories

UNWORTHY PLEASURE

She sat on the edge of her side of the bed, her clothes for the evening laid out next to her. Her shoulders sloped and her head hung, looking down at her clasp's hands on her thighs. A warm tear ran down her cheek and dripped onto her forearm.

Lost in her own thoughts, she didn't hear him walking up the stairs. He stood in the doorway, wearing black jeans and a white short sleeved shirt with a few buttons undone at the top. He was quiet as he watched her for a moment, admiring her body in her underwear. His gaze going from her long hair down her back past the clasp of her bra and down to the top of her knickers. He jumped as he heard her begin to cry, rushing to her side completely confused at the situation.

"Babe, what's the matter?' he asked quietly as he sat next to her grabbing her hands.

'I can't go' she muttered trying to hold back her sob.

'I don't understand. I thought you were excited to go out. We haven't been out to dinner just the two of us for ages." Sadness crossed his face and he as he made his statement.

'I can't go. Nothing fit's me anymore. I'm a mess. Why do you even want to be seen out with me anyway?' the tears were rolling down her face now, she couldn't lift her gaze to meet his. She felt guilty. Ashamed. Fat. Disgusting. Hate filled her body.

'Babe, you look amazing, but I know you won't believe me. Let me show you how incredible you are." He lifted up her hand and began to kiss the top of her hand, slowly making his way up her arm and kissed her neck, sending a shiver up her spine, causing her body to chill and her nipples go hard. Her shoulders relaxed as his hand held her thigh, gripping her slightly she moaned into his kisses.

"You are the most beautiful woman I have ever met" he whispered as he continued to kiss her neck. His words didn't sit right with what she thought about herself, she shook her head and tried to move away.

'You might not see it now babe but let me show you how to feel it tonight" his voice was soft but stern as his fingers grazed over her knickers. She couldn't help but part her legs and moan as his fingers moved away.

She looked up to meet his gaze, his eyes were hungry for her, and as he took in his face, she realized how much she missed having him. How much she missed his touch, his kisses, his cock. She felt something in her body waken to his touch, she reached closer to him and kisses him, allowing that hunger to spread through her and down to her pussy. She didn't care about anything other than how he made her feel. She needed him, his body on hers. He lay down bringing her with him, not letting her kiss go, but allowing his hands to move freely over her body, moving over her large breasts in her bra, down over her soft squishy belly and around to her large buttocks. He grabbed her arse pulling her body in closer to his, she felt his chest hairs tickling on her chest, a feeling she had forgotten. The feel of his hot body on her cool body felt like home, she wanted to be connected to him, she could feel his hard cock stuck, trapped in his jeans. Her hand fumbled around trying to undo his belt and buttons, she wanted to feel him, she wanted to feel his cock. He helped her to shimmy off his jeans and free his aching cock.

'You're not having me yet'. He smirked looking at her as she gazed down at his free dick. He leaned up and took off his shirt. Looking down at her he asked her to move up the bed, then began to free her breasts from her bra. He kissed over her breasts and licked her nipple on the way down to her belly. His fingers whipped off her knickers, baring her hairy pussy in all her glory to his hungry gaze. Her pussy was wet, he licked his lips as he could smell her desire for passion. She lay with her eyes closed, not wanting to see her husband's reaction to her body. Without warning her licked her pussy, one big, long, slow lick. She let out a huge moan as pleasure began to rush around her body. She had forgotten just how amazing this felt. He licked his lips, savoring the first taste of her, he'd hadn't tasted her in months. Then he kissed her lips before diving back in, he licked and sucked and licked some more. Her hands ran over his shoulders and face, founding his hair, running her fingers through his hair, her body began to jerk with every lick, the pleasure building up in her body. Her body began to rock with his flow, her hand left his body and found her nipples. She began to play with her nipples, the intense pleasure rushing from her nipples to her clit and back was enough to speed up her rhythm. He body began to move faster, her moans got louder, her body was submerged in pure pleasure, she could feel her pussy taking over her body, her pussy was loving the attention, loving the pleasure, loving her man licking and sucker at her. She felt nothing but amazing, her mind blank as she came undone in his mouth, he kept going sucking every bit of orgasm from her body, her body was shaking, her moans were louder than before, he held her to him by clutching her hips and licking like never before.

He let go as her body began to stop shaking. His face dripping in her cum her looked up at her. "You are fucking amazing' he smiled at her, she pulled his face up to meet hers. "No. You are fucking amazing' she whispered back before kissing him deeply, tasting herself on his tongue.

Their tongues danced with each other, their chests pressed into one another, he pushed his throbbing dick deep into her wet pussy with one thrust, causing her to gasp into his kiss.

Her body welcomed him in and without hesitation they began to move in sync. Clenching her pussy, she moaned as he thrust into her harder, she could feel her body responding to him, her nipples hard and aching she arched her back and gripped her right breast, her breasts felt so soft, large, and delicious in her hand. She brushed over her aching nipple and groaned with the immense pleasure ripping through her body down to her clit.

He looked down at her with pure lust, her body moving, her soft lips parting as she moaned with his every thrust, he loved making her moan, he loved seeing her body so free, sensual, and turned on.

She continued to touch her breast and ran her left hand down his chest "Fuck baby, you are so sexy" she whispered to him between deep moans.

"You have no idea how much I love seeing you naked" he said back, bending down and gently biting her neck.

He pulled her onto her side, then onto her front. Reached around to play with her clit and fucked her. Her legs began to tremble as he rubbed faster on her clit. Biting her pillow, she let out a scream as her body jerked and bucked back on his dick.

He fucked her harder and faster than before, keeping the pace up as she clenched hard around his dick and came, and he came in her.

The two flopped onto the bed, their breathes fast and heavy, but not wanting to part. He kissed her on her shoulder causing her body to feel electricity shoot down to her wet pussy.

"You are the most beautiful women I have ever seen" he said in-between kisses. "Let's just stay at home and enjoy each other all over again."

"Are you sure? I know you wanted to go out" she answered him back.

"I don't care what we do baby, I just want to be with you. I love you"

"I love you too" she smiled back at him.

STRIPPED

She took the glass off her friend and turned around to look at the rest of the club. It was still quiet in there, they were one of the first groups to arrive. The DJ was tucked away to the side and a huge stage filled the space, there were lots of empty seats in front of the stage. A Drag Queen was strutting around chatting to another group of women. They were all there for cheap cocktails and male strippers.

It wasn't long before the club got very busy, there were men and women everywhere. Drunk and hungry to see naked men.

She sat back and began to enjoy the show, guy after guy came out on the stage and did there performance.

"I'm just popping to the toilet" she whispered to her friend. As she got up to go the next song came on, she looked back to check out the guy. 'Holy Shit' she muttered to herself before walking into the wall. He stared right at her and she instantly felt herself get wet and flustered straight away. She ran into the bathroom to calm herself down.

When she came out the bathroom, he had finished his show and was nowhere to be seen. She made her way back to her seat. "Are you okay?" her friend asked.

"Yeah why?" she replied.

"You walked into the wall" she laughed.

"Shit, you saw that?"

"Yeah, he was staring at the back, so I turned around to look and saw you walk into the wall. He's fit, isn't he?! And his dick looks huge." She laughed.

After the show the group of girls were all up dancing and drinks were flowing. The next thing a hand ran up her leg and around to her waist, then pulled her in tight into a body. She pulled away and turned around and saw the stripper stood smiling at her. His blue eyes were capturing her soul, she instantly felt a pull to move back to his body. To be all over his body. To be naked and riding his dick.

After an hour of being in the club, she couldn't take it anymore and left to go back to the hotel with him.

As they got into the lift, he picked her up with one arm and pushed her back into the cold metal. Feeling the heat off his body and the cold metal her nipples hardened. His tongue was deep in her mouth, hungry for each other, her hands ran through his hair, and down over his shoulders. When the lift stopped, he placed her back down on the floor and held her hand to walk out, following her to the hotel room.

As soon as he shut the door behind him, he moved over to her and slowly kissed her shoulders as he unzipped her dress and let it fall to the floor.

His lips moved down to the tops of her breasts, as he undid her bra freeing her perk small breast. He bent down on one knee and kissed her torso, her body shivered with every gentle kiss. Her pussy getting wetter as he slowly made his way down to her knickers. His hands grabbing her arse cheeks he pulls her pussy to his face and breathes in her scent. She lets out a gentle moan as she longs for him to rip her knickers off and lick her aching clit.

He parts her legs and begins to kiss her thighs; her pussy begins to pulsate as she can feel the warmth off his face. Her body arches as she tries to move herself closer to his mouth, longing for him to lick her wet pussy.

He continues to kiss her thigh, with a smirk on his face as he can smell her turn on. He looks up at her face, their eyes lock for a moment. Their souls dancing as though they have known each other for a lifetime. Then he breaks their connection and dives straight into her pussy. There was no warning, just eagerly he was licking her pussy. Like forbidden fruit, he ate, and ate. Her body erupted. She couldn't contain herself anymore and came eagerly on his tongue, he didn't stop. Her body kept cuming, and cuming. She screamed in pure delight as her body tingled all over.

When she finally gained control over herself, he held her hand and pulled her up onto her feet. Her legs were trembling as he stood behind her and whispered, "Now I'm going to fuck you in the shower" and picked her up around her waist.

He placed her down in the walk-in shower and turned on the water. The hot water was soothing but stung on the area's where he had been kissing and biting, she stood under the shower head and allowed her whole body to feel the soothing from the water, as he began to kiss her again. The water running down their faces, gasping for air but not wanting to leave his kiss. He turned her around and pressed her breasts into the cold tiles. Her nipples hardened to the chill and goose bumps ran down her stomach to her pussy. Her tugged on her hair and separated her legs to give him access to her pussy. She wanted to feel him deep inside her, she moaned in the anticipation of him entering her, her pushed her arse out towards him and her breasts firmly placed on the tiles, she readied herself. She wanted him; her pussy wanted him. She could feel his hard cock behind her, as he pressed himself against her, kissing down her neck and shoulders. He pushed his hard cock inside her, her pussy welcomed him in, and purred with pure delight as her entire body lit up.

HARDER

The day had been long, her body ached as exhaustion tried to take over. Her feet ached from walking around all day in her heels. She opened her front door, threw her bag on the side, dropped her coat over the back of the sofa and made her way into the kitchen. She checked the fridge and there was no food, nothing in the cupboards, so decided to call for a take-away. Poured herself a glass of wine and began to run a bath.

The hot water soothed her aching body, the bubbles feeling soft against her skin. Her legs and boobs submerged under the water, she relaxed. Music played quietly in the background and candles lit the bathroom.

She could feel herself slipping in and out of sleep, until the doorbell went.

Completely forgetting she had ordered a takeaway she jumped out of the bath grabbing the closest towel she could find and made her way to the door. She whipped open the front door to find her last booty call stood in her doorway with the bag of food and a huge grin on his face. He looked her up and down. She noticed he kept looking down towards her pussy. She looked down and realised she had only picked up the hand towel off the side, not her bath towel and her pussy was on show to the word. "I will bring this in for you" he said as he walked past her towards the kitchen.

He grabbed himself a glass of wine, whilst she ran into the bathroom and got her dressing gown on.

"What the hell are you doing here?" she said walking into the kitchen.

"I saw the delivery guy walking up to your house, so told him it was ours and I thought I'd treat you" he smirked back.

"Treat me? With my own food?" she snarled at him.

"I thought I'd give you something else, but you can have your food first. You need your energy." He brushed a hair off her face and kissed the top of her head.

"fuck" she thought.

Work had been stressful, and she hadn't had sex since she last slept with him over 3 weeks ago. She felt all of her body relax when he kissed her head. She had been so busy she had forgotten what it felt like to relax, to feel into her body, to cum.

He took her hand and led her to the sofa. She straddled his lap, their kisses becoming more and more frantic. Wanting each other. Remembering each other. She pulled his shirt off, and ran her hand down his smooth pecs, how she missed seeing his muscles dance under the flickering of candlelight. Her dressing gown slipped off her shoulder, releasing one of her breasts, she leaned forward and continued to kiss him, their chests touching, her nipple hardening on his pec. He pulled her dressing gown off her other shoulder, releasing both her pert breasts. He cupped one of her small breasts in his large hand, and gentle massaged it and her nipple between his fingers. She let out a moan "Fuck, I've missed that" she whispered.

He dropped her dressing gown to the floor, leaving her naked on his lap. In one sharp move he spanked her arse then pulled her in close to him so she could feel the pleasure rush up her body. Then he did the same on the other side. Spanking her hard, then playing with her nipple on the opposite side. Her body was a whirlwind of pleasure and heat, rushing and soaring through her body.

"This is for making me wait to have you again" he growled down her ear and spanked her arse again, and again, and again. The heat rushed straight to her pussy as she let out a moan.

He pulled one of her legs up onto his shoulder and began to lick her pussy. "Holy fuck" she moaned, she used one hand to steady herself and one hand to undo his jeans. She wanted to ride him, to fuck him, to cum all over his cock. Pulling her arse closer to him he kept licking and eating her pussy. Like a wild beast, he wouldn't stop until he got what he wanted. He held her in to him as her body began to jerk as her orgasm came from nowhere and exploded in his mouth, he didn't let go until she pulled herself off his face. His eyes were dark, he wanted more. He wriggled his jeans down and freed his hard cock. With one hard thrust he was deep inside her. They both moaned as his pulsating cock filled her. She had forgotten how big he was, how he took up every bit of room she had, how his cock fitted her perfectly.

She began to ride him, back and forth, he grabbed her arse and began to help her move faster. Pulling her back and forth they built up momentum. Her body began to tingle and her nipples hardened. He began to bite and suck on her left nipple whilst pulling and twisting on her other nipple. She let out a huge moan, she could feel it on her clit as he licked and tugged her nipples. She began to feel his shoulders, down over his pec's, his hard muscles turning her on even more. Then he spanked her again. "Harder" she moaned. "Fuck me harder" he spanked her again and pulled her back and forth. "Harder, fuck me" she begged him. He picked her up off him and placed her on her knees on the edge of the sofa. Grabbing a fist full of her hair, he fucked her. Faster. Harder.

"Fuck, yes" she screamed whilst playing with her clit.

He smacked her arse in perfect timing with his thrusting, as she rubbed her clit.

"I'm going to cum" she screamed as he kept fucking her.

"Don't stop" she plead, "don't stop".

Her body tingled from head to toe as she came on his dick, he kept fucking her as she exploded, until he came too.

ABOUT THE AUTHOR

Jessica is a wife, mother, foster carer and military veteran.
With a passion for sex, her past sexual encounters and deep
connection with her husband she has a vast understanding and
wisdom connected to all thing sex, passion, pleasure but also pain,
suffering, and heart ache.
The author has dedicated her life to helping other women find deeper
personal connections and enjoy a life filled with orgasms, pleasure,
and a massive bank account.
She does this via 1:1 sessions online and group sessions.

Printed in Great Britain
by Amazon

75755489R00068